Accessing England's Protected Wreck Sites

Guidance Notes for Divers and Archaeologists

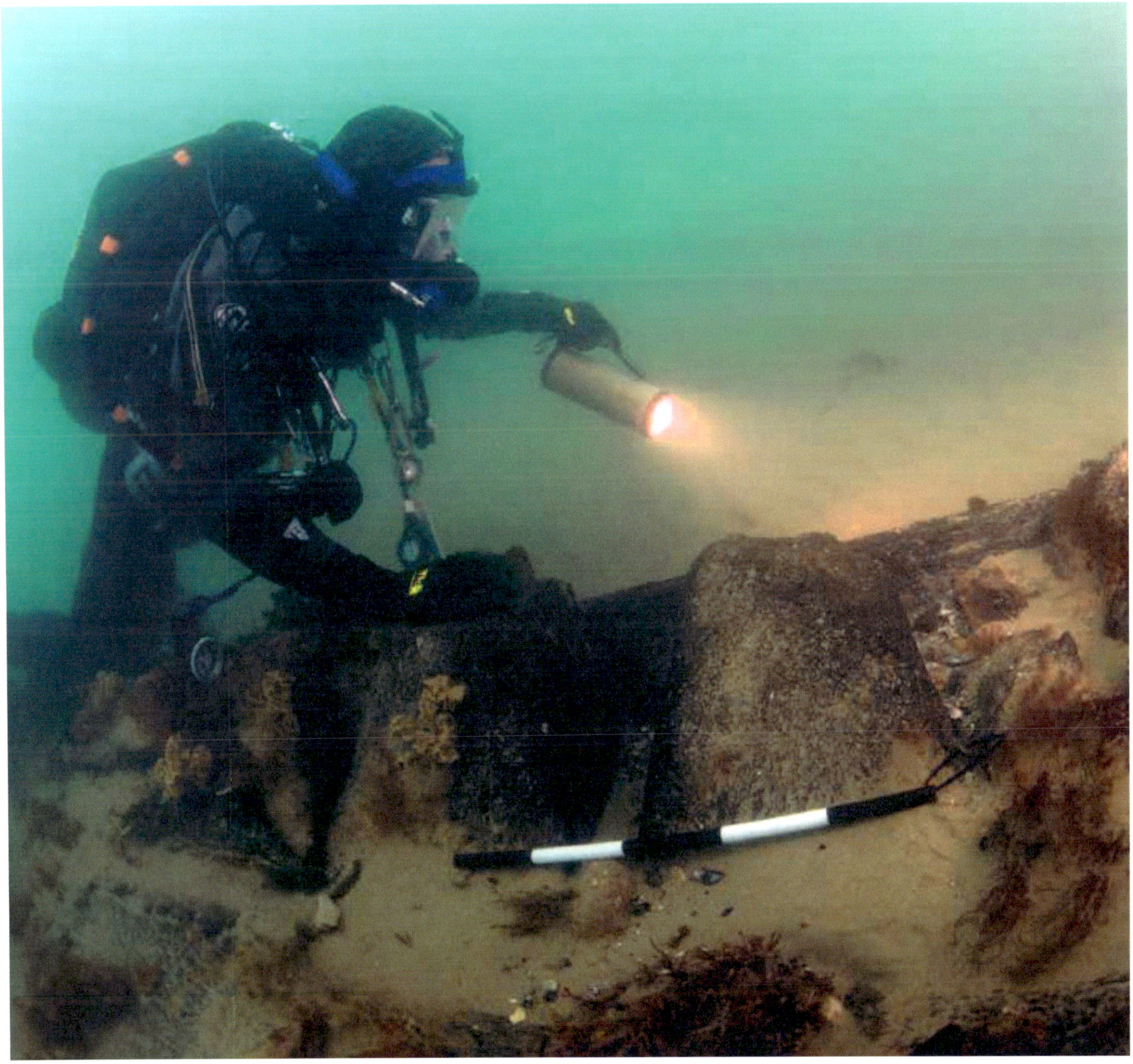

Summary

The diversity of England's Protected Wreck Sites reflects the wealth of maritime heritage preserved under the sea and around our coast. These sites provide a valuable source of evidence for a wide range of past activities, and not just of those on or in the sea.

These guidelines are intended to support individuals or groups wishing to access and/or develop projects on wreck sites designated under Section 1 of the *Protection of Wrecks Act* 1973 in the English Territorial Sea.

The role of a voluntary Licensee and his or her team is essential to the system that helps manage the most significant historic wrecks in our territorial sea. As Licensees are effectively voluntary custodians for these important sites; this has been recognised by Historic England awarding Affiliated Volunteer Status to Licensees and their teams (Figure 2).

This guidance has been updated to reflect changes to the way the protected wreck licensing system is administered, recognise the *Marine and Coastal Access Act* 2009 and publication of the *UK Marine Policy Statement* in 2011.

The guidance forms the approach recommended for work on all historic wreck sites in England, not just those designated under the *Protection of Wrecks Act* 1973.

These guidelines were prepared by Mark Dunkley (Maritime Designation Adviser) and Alison James (Maritime Archaeologist) at Historic England. Comments and suggestions for further improvements are welcome: alison.james@HistoricEngland.org.uk

This document is based on work initiated by Annabel Lawrence and Jesse Ransley. It includes contributions from Duncan Brown, Gill Campbell, Mark Harrison and Angela Middleton. The authors are grateful for comments received on early drafts of this guidance, in particular from the Historic England Standards and Guidelines Manager.

First published by English Heritage August 2010.
This edition published by Historic England October 2015.
All images © Historic England unless otherwise stated.

https://www.historicengland.org.uk/advice/planning/consents/protected-wreck-sites/

Front cover: A diver explores HMS *Invincible*.
Image: Mike Pitts and Pascoe Archaeology Services.

Contents

Introduction............................1		**2**	**Planning a Project...............16**	
The scope of these guidelines 1		2.1	Site ownership, location and administrative responsibility...................16	
General principles of approach 1		2.2	Intrusive and non-intrusive investigation......................16	
Protected Wreck Sites 2		2.3	Dive Trails 18	
Responsibilities of Historic England 3		2.4	Fieldwork safety..19	
Historic Wrecks Panel..3		2.5	Environmental considerations..................21	
Contract for Archaeological Services 3		2.6	Funding and training 22	
		2.7	Producing a Project Design 23	

1	**Applying for a Licence 4**		**3**	**During a Project....................24**
1.1	Protected Wreck Site Licences....................4		3.1	Fieldwork: data collection 24
1.2	The role of a Licensee..................................7		3.2	Dealing with finds 25
1.3	Affiliated Volunteer Status 9		3.4	Site Security and liaison 28
1.4	Applying for a licence 9		3.5	Monitoring and site restitution................30
1.5	Recovery of material....................................10			
1.6	Disturbance of the seabed through excavation......................................10		**4**	**Reporting, Archiving and Dissemination 31**
1.7	Geophysical Survey 12		4.1	Submitting Licensee reports.....................31
1.8	Referees 13		4.2	The project archive....................................32
1.10	Nominated Archaeologists........................13		4.3	Publication 32
1.12	Association of Protected Wreck Licensees..15			

5 Where to Get Advice 33

5.1 References and further reading 33
5.2 Useful contacts 34
5.3 Useful acronyms 35

6 Appendices 36

6.1 Annex to the 2001 UNESCO Convention on the Protection of the Underwater Cultural Heritage...36
I General principles.......................................36
II Project design 37
III Preliminary work 37
IV Project objective, methodology and techniques 38
V Funding 38
VI Project duration – timetable 38
VII Competence and qualifications 38
VIII Conservation and site management 38
IX Documentation 38
X Safety 38
XI Environment 38
XII Reporting 39
XIII Curation of project archives 39
XIV Dissemination 39
6.2 Standard licence conditions.....................40
6.3 Licensee's annual report 41

Introduction

The scope of these guidelines

This document provides guidance for individuals or groups wishing to access and/or develop projects on wreck sites designated under Section 1 of the *Protection of Wrecks Act* 1973 in the English Territorial Sea, as well as being the recommended approach for work on all historic wreck sites in England. Access to such sites is enabled through a licensing system administered by Historic England on behalf of the Department for Culture, Media and Sport (DCMS). Authorisation to access a Protected Wreck Site is at the discretion of the Secretary of State for Culture, Media & Sport.

Additional information on investigative archaeological projects can be found in Historic England's *MoRPHE Project Planning Notes* and guidelines.

General principles of approach

The UK Government has adopted the Annex to the 2001 UNESCO *Convention on the Protection of the Underwater Cultural Heritage* as being best practice for archaeology. This Annex (reproduced in Appendix 1) comprises a series of ethical rules concerning activities directed at underwater cultural heritage, which provide objective standards by which to assess the appropriateness of actions in respect to archaeology underwater. All individuals licensed to access a Protected Wreck Site agree to uphold the general principles of the Rules annexed to the 2001 Convention. The *UK Marine Policy Statement* recognises that heritage assets should be conserved in a manner appropriate and proportionate to their significance. This is further underpinned by highlighting the need to record and advance our understanding of heritage assets for this and future generations. The *UK Marine Policy Statement* states that the historic environment represents a unique aspect of our cultural heritage and is a finite and often irreplaceable resource that can be vulnerable to a range of human activities. As such, these guidelines are intended to assist those interested in investigating, recording and preserving our past.

> The "high level of non-vocational involvement should be regarded as an asset to the discipline, as there is demonstrably a greater requirement for survey and recording than can possibly be accomplished by professional archaeologists" (*Taking to the Water*, English Heritage 2006).

Figure 1: A diving archaeologist prepares to enter the water to undertake a site assessment on behalf of Historic England.
Image: Wessex Archaeology, © Crown Copyright.

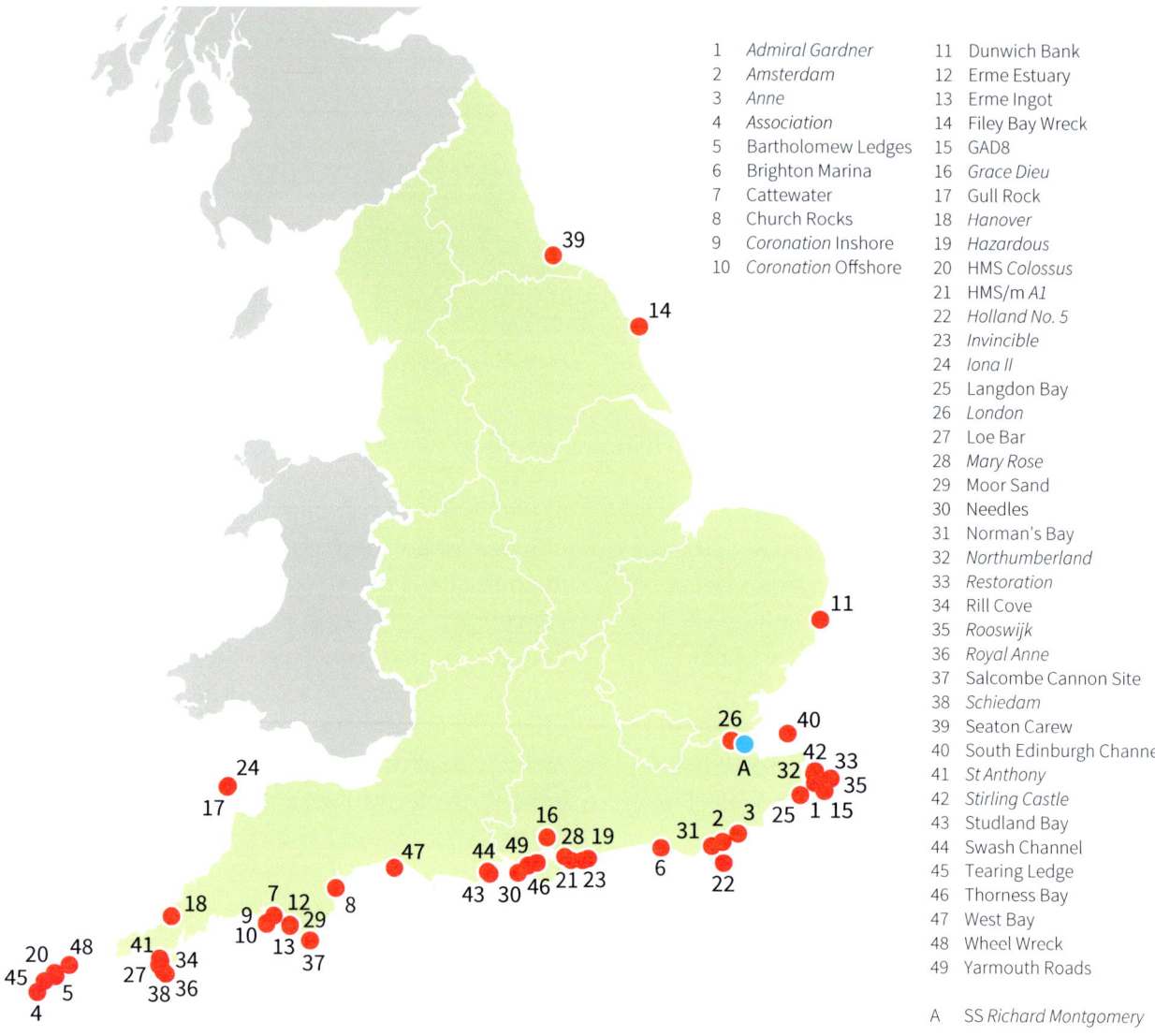

Figure 2: England's Protected Wreck Sites (January 2016).

Protected Wreck Sites

Designation of important historic wreck sites in the Territorial Seas of England, Wales and Northern Ireland occurs under Section 1 of the *Protection of Wrecks Act* 1973, which enables the Government to control investigations of wreck sites and the adjacent seabed (relevant sections of the Act has since been repealed in Scotland). Designated sites under Section 1 of the Act are identified as being those likely to contain the remains of a vessel, or its contents, which are of historical, artistic or archaeological importance.

Historic England has published a designation selection guide explaining the criteria used to assess the significance of a wreck site which is being considered for designation. Historic England has also produced *Ships and Boats: Prehistory to 1840* and *Ships and Boats: 1840-1950* as expert yet accessible introductions to significant vessel types. These documents are all available to download from the Historic England website.

The purpose of designation is to capture a representative sample of our nationally important historical and archaeological resource where statutory protection is deemed to be the most appropriate mechanism to secure their long-term preservation for this and future generations. The designated wreck sites in England represent a small percentage of the many hundreds of known sites around the English coastline and in our seas. Anyone may apply for a historic wreck site to be designated under the terms of the *Protection of Wrecks Act* 1973; application forms can be filled in on-line.

The *Protection of Wrecks Act* 1973 does not prohibit access to designated wrecks; rather, it controls activities so that designated wrecks are not put at risk from undisciplined actions or unauthorised investigation. A copy of the *Protection of Wrecks Act* 1973 can be obtained from www.opsi.gov.uk. Further information on Protected Wreck Sites and England's Maritime Archaeology is available from Historic England.

Section 2 of the *Protection of Wrecks Act* 1973 governs restrictions in relation to dangerous wrecks. This Section of the Act is administered by the Maritime and Coastguard Agency.

Responsibilities of Historic England

Historic England's specific responsibilities to maritime archaeological sites derive from the *National Heritage Act* 2002, which modified strategic functions to include:

- securing the preservation of ancient monuments in, on or under the seabed; **and**

- promoting the public's enjoyment of, and advancing their knowledge of ancient monuments in, on or under the seabed

The 2002 Act also enabled the Secretary of State for Culture, Media and Sport to transfer administrative functions (particularly with regard to licensing access) relating to the *Protection of Wrecks Act* 1973 to Historic England. Historic England's responsibilities in relation to designated wrecks also derive from the *National Heritage Act* 2002, whereby Historic England is able to grant-aid projects in relation to Protected Wreck Sites.

Historic Wrecks Panel

Historic England's Historic Wrecks Panel replaced the Advisory Committee on Historic Wreck Sites in 2011, in relation to England. The Panel advises staff on specialist issues of policy and practice related to complex, contentious and high profile wreck sites in UK territorial waters adjacent to England and in UK controlled waters adjacent to England and licensing in UK territorial waters adjacent to England, as appropriate.

Contract for Archaeological Services

When considering an application for designation, Historic England is assisted by a team of contract diving archaeologists.

The overall aim of the contract is to provide quality information to Historic England to enable the protection and management of heritage assets in a manner appropriate to their significance, both at the coast and within English territorial waters. This is achieved through the provision and deployment of an array of archaeological field capabilities including, but not limited to, desk-based assessment, diver-based investigation and remote sensing in order to:

- Undertake specific assessment and/or targeted investigation as directed by Historic England, **and**

- Maintain and deliver an archive of primary site data and reports to include site reports, documentary research and logs, digital data including GIS information, bathymetry and imagery

1 Applying for a Licence

1.1 Protected Wreck Site Licences

Authorised access to England's Protected Wreck Sites is facilitated through a licensing scheme administered by Historic England on behalf of DCMS. In England, licences enabling access are subject to the authorisation of the Secretary of State for Culture, Media and Sport. Archaeology should be accessible to all and, mindful of the rights of individuals to engage with our shared heritage (coupled with their diving competence), anyone may apply to access a Protected Wreck Site.

Individuals and/or groups wishing to simply visit and/or undertake archaeological activities (including some types of remote sensing) on Protected Wreck Sites may only do so with an appropriate licence.

In autumn 2015 the licensing process was amended to move from four different types of licence to just one, framed by conditions that are relevant to the proposed activities. This change does not alter the processes for approving and issuing licences but rather amends the type of licence issued to make it fit for purpose with current archaeological techniques and to reflect the broad range of reasons for which people seek to access protected wreck sites. The change also introduced the term 'Principal Licensee' who is the main licence holder and, usually, the applicant.

A **Licensee** is a voluntary custodian of the site. It is important to note that the role of Licensee for a Protected Wreck Site does not confer ownership or salvage rights.

Although anyone can apply to access a Protected Wreck Site, a licence will only be authorised by DCMS if it will be of benefit to the care, understanding or public appreciation of the site. On some designated wrecks, licences may be granted to more than one individual in a year, but these licences will be conditional on the co-operation of individual licence holders (Licensees) and the program of proposed activity being integrated and mutually beneficial.

Although archaeological investigations will inevitably be undertaken by a team, licences are issued to a named individual (the Principal Licensee) who takes sole responsibility for the on-site activities of everyone in that team. Clubs or groups interested in undertaking authorised activities will have to decide who is to be the Principal Licensee. Certain types of licence will also require a named archaeologist to work with the team; a named archaeologist is referred to as the Nominated Archaeologist, which is usually a voluntary role. In all cases, Historic England acts as the default archaeological advisor.

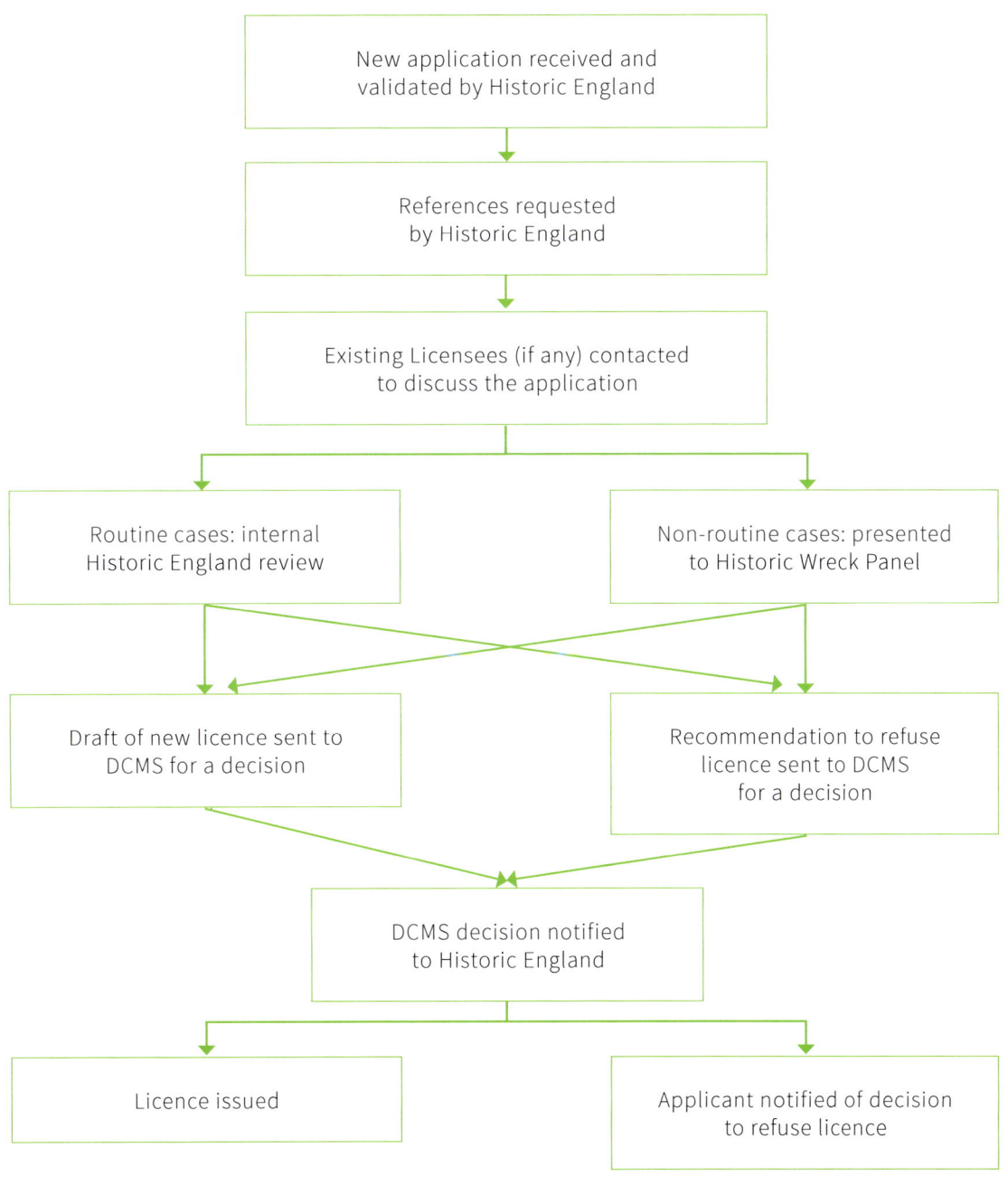

Figure 3: The licence application process.

Figure 4: The Licensee and members of the licensed team working alongside an archaeological dive team during the #LondonWreck1665 project.
Image: Luke Mair

Generally speaking licences will only be issued by the Secretary of State to people who are considered:

- to be competent, and properly equipped, to carry out operations appropriate to the historical and archaeological importance of any wreck lying in a restricted area and of any objects contained or formerly contained in a wreck as defined under the *Protection of Wrecks Act* 1973; **and**

- to have any other legitimate reason for doing things in the area that can only be done with a licence

All applications requesting access to Protected Wreck Sites are appraised on merit. All applicants are therefore invited to contact Historic England to discuss proposed projects before submitting a formal application (see Section 5 for contact details).

Application forms to access a Protected Wreck Site can be filled in on-line or downloaded from Historic England. Historic England will always provide additional guidance, upon request, to anyone wishing to apply for a licence to access a designated wreck.

1.2 The role of a Licensee

The role of a voluntary Licensee and their team is essential to the system that helps to manage the most significant historic wrecks in UK territorial waters (Figure 5). These sites provide valuable evidence for a wide range of past activities, and not just those on or in the sea. The diversity of Protected Wreck Sites indicates the wealth of maritime information preserved under the sea and around the coast of the UK.

The incentives for investigating and caring for a nationally important historic wreck are broad: Licensees and their work have been featured on national television and in the national press, presented papers at conferences, contributed to local, regional and national outreach events, published their work in archaeological journals and even written booklets, monographs and developed websites. The experience can be very rewarding, but it is important to note that Licensees also acquire a high level of responsibility. As activities within the designated area are limited to those agreed with Historic England and covered by the licence, the duties of a Licensee will vary depending on the work that is taking place and the conditions of the licence (see Appendix 2).

Licensees are not required to hold formal archaeological qualifications, but are expected to have a technical knowledge of archaeological principles and practice. Further, Licensees are expected to be competent to undertake and complete their proposed activity, including the preparation of a written report of results, and the preparation of archives as indicated below, although Historic England recognises that 'competence' differs from 'qualification' (a quality or accomplishment) in that competence is simply the ability to do a task (NAS 2009).

Figure 5: Protected wreck sites can generate a lot of publicity as was the case with the gun carriage from the *London*.

All Licensees are required to do the following:

- Comply with the conditions of their licence

- Uphold archaeological principles (including the Rules annexed to the 2001 UNESCO *Convention on the Protection of the Underwater Cultural Heritage*)

- Take the lead in maintaining close contact with the Nominated Archaeologist and with Historic England

- Ensure that licensed activities are undertaken safely and by competent people

- Produce a yearly report on their work on the site to Historic England

Principal Licensees are responsible for, and must manage, on-site activity during all operations under their licence. However, Historic England recognises that it is not practical, or indeed always possible, for a Principal Licensee to be on site at all times. The Principal Licensee can add a number of named additional Licensees who are responsible on-site when the Principal Licensee is not present. They must be named on the licence and can be added during the initial application or by notifying Historic England.

Previously the licencing process required that the names of all divers must be listed in the schedule accompanying the licence, usually referred to as 'Named Divers'. In order to reduce the burden of paperwork on Licensees, and to allow diving to occur at short notice, the license now only needs to carry the name of the Licensees. The Licensees may take additional divers on dives under and in accordance with the terms of their licence without prior notification to Historic England. Licensees will therefore no longer have to provide a list of additional divers when applying for a licence or apply for a

Figure 6: Becoming a Licensee and an affiliated volunteer can be an enjoyable experience.
Image: Mark Beattie Edwards.

Figure 7: Work, such as this Historic England funded excavation on the *London*, which disturbs the seabed or involves the recovery of material will require a full Project Design.

---

variation to a licence to include further divers. Historic England will, however, continue to collect the names of divers who have visited a site under a licence at set intervals throughout the year. It is the responsibility of the Principal Licensee to ensure a list of names is maintained and made available to Historic England upon request.

1.3 Affiliated Volunteer Status

All Licensees, Team Members and Nominated Archaeologists on Protected Wreck Site Licences are eligible to be Affiliated Volunteers of Historic England if they fulfil the criteria set out by Historic England. Licensees dive protected wreck sites to gather vital information on behalf of Historic England without payment. Historic England values and appreciates the full worth of Licensees and classifies them as Affiliated Volunteers because they give their time and expertise to Historic England free of charge. As such, affiliated volunteers will be recognised by Historic England through the commitments outlined in the Historic England Volunteer Policy, with the exception of travel and insurance arrangements which are overridden by the conditions on the license. Historic England will work with affiliated volunteers in order to accommodate our organisational policies and procedures related to volunteering.

Affiliated volunteers are subject to the conditions on the license on which they are named; this classification does not affect health, safety and legal responsibilities. For the avoidance of doubt, affiliated volunteers are not employees or members of staff and it is not intended that they should be.

1.4 Applying for a licence

Before licences are issued and before any authorised activity takes place on a Protected Wreck Site, it is important for Historic England and DCMS to know what is proposed and why; proposals should be discussed with a Nominated Archaeologist and with Historic England as early as possible, so that appropriate guidance can be given against the scope of proposed activities. All licences therefore include standard conditions. Applying to visit a site may be the first stage before applying for future further licences.

Where proposed activities will disturb the sea bed or include the recovery of any material Historic England will require the submission of an accompanying Project Design; it is important that a detailed project plan and explanation of what is to be undertaken, and how, is prepared. More detailed, and recommended, advice on project design specification can be found in Appendix 1 as well as the Historic England publication *Management of Research Projects in the Historic Environment: The MoRPHE Project Managers' Guide* (Historic England 2015b). It is recommended that project designs to accompany applications follow this guidance.

Licences are granted on the understanding that information obtained as a result of authorised activity will be available and accessible to the public. Consequently, Licensees are required to deposit the project archive of work undertaken on any designated wreck in an appropriate repository and to ensure that there are no copyright restraints upon Third Party use of such material for non-commercial purposes. Additional information on archiving is set out later in these guidelines.

The application process is compliant to *European Union Services Directive* (Directive 2006/123/EC).

1.5 Recovery of material

An application to allow the recovery of material will not normally be recommended by Historic England to the Secretary of State unless a strong case is made that the recovery of exposed artefacts is appropriate (Figure 8). Any application will need to:

(a) provide a Project Design indicating the reasons and methodology for recovery, and provide detail on conservation measures in place to receive the material; and

(b) provide evidence of an agreement-in-principle that a museum is willing to house the collection of the recovered material (subject to the investigations of the Receiver of Wreck)

Further, Historic England encourages Licensees to waive their rights to a salvage award (under the *Merchant Shipping Act* 1995) in favour of an appropriate museum in recognition of the special historic, archaeological, architectural or artistic interest of the site, consistent with advice given in *Our Portable Past* (English Heritage 2006a). Recovered finds are subject to the controls of the *Merchant Shipping Act* 1995. The Receiver of Wreck has a policy of trying to keep historic material together and offering it to registered museums but there is no guarantee that an appropriate museum will have the resources to acquire and conserve material from a wreck site. Therefore it is essential that conservation and long-term curation of any recovered material is considered in the Project Design for any project that includes the proposed recovery of material.

1.6 Disturbance of the seabed through excavation

An individual applying for a licence for work that will disturb the seabed will be required to:

(a) provide a Project Design indicating the reasons and methodology for recovery and provide detail on conservation measures in place to receive the material;

(b) provide evidence of an agreement-in-principle that a museum is willing to house the collection of the recovered material (subject to the investigations of the Receiver of Wreck); **and**

(c) provide evidence that all necessary consents will be sought prior to work commencing

In most cases, the direction of excavation and/or sampling activities would have to be under the total control of an appropriately qualified and experienced Nominated Archaeologist. The Nominated Archaeologist would need to be involved in preparation of a Project Design for the intended investigation and would normally need to be on site for most of the time the work was taking place.

Figure 8: Archaeologists excavate the wreck of HMS *Colossus*.
Image: CISMAS

Example activities that might take place on a Protected Wreck Site	PWA licence required?	Project Design required?
Geophysical Survey	No (in most but not all cases)	n/a
Site Visit Photography Videography Visual monitoring Measured survey Photographic survey Compilation of site plans Recording of seabed topography Ecological survey	Yes	No Project Design required in most cases
Installation of dive trail stations Installation of sandbags or other protective material Recovery of high risk items exposed on the seabed	Yes	Yes
Controlled removal of sediments Collection of samples for research		

Figure 9: Types of activities that might take place on sites and the requirement for an accompanying Project Design.

1.7 Geophysical Survey

Most geophysical survey projects will not require a licence under the *Protection of Wrecks Act* 1973. However, Historic England would ask that people planning such projects notify us of their intentions and the likely dates of any survey beforehand. This can be done by completing the online form. This helps to ensure that all stakeholders for a site are aware of the planned work and avoids operations occurring simultaneously. There are a small number of cases where a licence might be required, for example during sector scanning sonar survey work there is the requirement to place a frame on the seabed and this would require a license under the *Protection of Wrecks Act*. If you are unsure, or would like to discuss your planned work, then please consult Historic England.

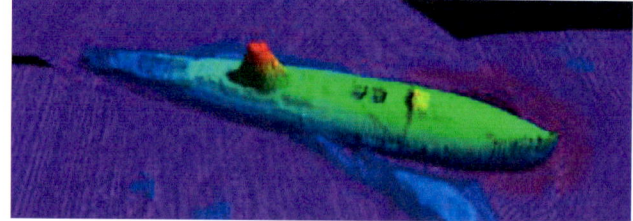

Figure 10: Geophysical survey, such as this Multibeam on HMS/m *A1*, will not require a licence in most cases.
Image: MSDS Marine.

1.8 Referees

Applicants are required to provide the names of two referees (plus an additional two referees for Nominated Archaeologists). Referees must be able to confirm the identity, experience and qualifications of the applicant and/or Nominated Archaeologist. The referee should also include comment on the applicant's adherence to the Rules annexed to the 2001 *Convention on the Protection of Underwater Cultural Heritage*. Through this process the Historic England can advise the Secretary of State that the applicant is sufficiently competent to be recommended a licence or to act as a Nominated Archaeologist.

To avoid unnecessary administration, references will only be sought when a new person applies for a licence, or when an existing Licensee applies for a licence that entails more intrusive work than on his or her existing or previous licence(s).

> **Referees** should not be named without their permission and cannot be listed as a named diver on the application form. Referees must not be employees of Historic England.

1.9 Duration of licences

Licences are normally valid from the date of issue to the following end of November. Where an existing licence is due to expire, the Principal Licensee may re-apply for the continuation of the same licence using a Licence Renewal Form. It is important to note that licences can be varied or revoked by the Secretary of State at any time, after giving not less that one week's notice to the Licensee.

1.10 Nominated Archaeologists

Where appointed by a Licensee, the level of input of a voluntary Nominated Archaeologist will depend on the type of activities being licensed, the experience of the project team and personal availability. In most instances where the licensed activity is non-intrusive, the Nominated Archaeologist may not need to take any formal responsibility for the archaeological work, but he or she would be expected to provide advice on strategy and document preparation and must be available to give general archaeological advice. If you do not know how to find an appropriate archaeologist, please contact Historic England.

It is the Licensee's responsibility to maintain regular contact with the Nominated Archaeologist. Nominated Archaeologists should be competent to provide archaeological advice appropriate for the type of licence held. They may not necessarily be able to dive, but where intrusive investigations are taking place, this would normally be a requirement. Nominated Archaeologists are expected to comply with established archaeological Codes of Conduct and have the appropriate measure of qualifications and experience to match the advice being given. Nominated Archaeologists should also acquire a sound knowledge of legislation, standards and guidance applicable to maritime archaeology. It is permissible for a Licensee and Nominated Archaeologist to be the same individual.

Although Nominated Archaeologists advising on some licences may not need to visit or dive the site, it often helps; and it is imperative that no artefact is recovered without prior, specific consultation with the Nominated Archaeologist. The archaeologists need to make themselves available for telephone consultation or for pre-arranged meetings at intervals appropriate to the complexity of the work. On some sites this might be once every day while work is taking place, but it is more likely to be weekly, and less frequently when there is no on-going site activity.

Where archaeological material is exposed on the surface of the seabed, and a licence is issued to recover items, the Nominated Archaeologist will need to be more closely involved. The archaeologist must help to formulate the strategy so that recovery can take place without unnecessary disturbance of the underlying material, and advise on post-recovery procedures.

On-site presence may not be essential but it is obviously useful. Material should not be raised before the Nominated Archaeologist has discussed and agreed the need, strategy and post-recovery stabilisation, conservation and deposition plan with the Licensee.

The amount of time a Nominated Archaeologist needs to make available to a project will vary considerably from site to site and team to team. The archaeologist would need to have input into the recording and interpretation of the distribution of material or topographical information, and would be expected to be involved in the production of the reports. The archaeologist may also need to make sure the Licensee is following conservation advice.

Where a licence is issued that permits the disturbance of the seabed and/or the recovery of material, the Nominated Archaeologist will need to take total control of the archaeological side of the project. When controlling intrusive work on a designated site, he or she should have a close working relationship with the Licensee and a good working relationship with the whole team.

The Nominated Archaeologist should be on site for most of the time disturbance is taking place, unless the site is suitable for supervision by someone with proven archaeological experience in excavation techniques. This person will need to be able to identify and record archaeological contexts, features and objects as they appear, and also manage the flow of information and objects as they come to the surface. This should be discussed in the Project Design and the experience and proposed responsibilities of this person should be clearly laid out.

The archaeologist should be experienced and confident enough to argue the archaeological case wherever necessary. This does not mean that they need vast experience of underwater excavation, although that always helps. What is primarily required is the ability to transfer the basic archaeological procedures used on land to the underwater environment and communicate this expertise to the project team. Sometimes the archaeologist will have less diving experience than the Licensee and so safety and non-archaeological operational activities may be best left to the Licensee. If the archaeologist has any concerns over safety or diving procedures, these concerns should be expressed to the Licensee.

Nominated Archaeologists have the authority to stop work on sites if they have serious concerns regarding inappropriate activities.

1.11 Communication with Licensees

Historic England regularly issues information to Licensees and to Nominated Archaeologists through a Licensee e-Bulletin. This electronic newsletter provides information on public policy, links to new initiatives and other relevant matters for Licensees to forward to their respective teams. Licensees are invited to provide material of interest to other project teams and are also invited to participate in a LinkedIn group.

Historic England also issue updates and news items through Twitter using the username @HEMaritime. Licensees and all divers visiting protected wreck sites are encouraged to post photos of their visits to the sites to the Historic England Maritime Archaeology Flickr stream: www.flickr.com/groups/ehmaritime

It is worth noting that the Chartered Institute for Archaeologists Maritime Affairs Group (CIfA MAG) has developed an on-line blog that also disseminates maritime archaeological information. Subscription to the blog is free and is a useful way to keep informed about related developments, see: ifamag.wordpress.com

Historic England has also developed on-line access to site reports derived from the Archaeological Contractor. These reports indicate some of the most recent research being undertaken on many of the designated wrecks.

It is also important for the Licensee to maintain communication with their team members so that information is shared, all participants are kept informed and the results of research by any member are relayed effectively to everyone involved with the project.

1.12 Association of Protected Wreck Licensees

The Association of Protected Wreck Licensees (APWL) was established in 2013 as a forum to facilitate open communication, discussion, collaboration and co-operation within the community of avocational and professional archaeologists who work on, survey, monitor and research the wreck sites around the UK coastline that are protected by law through designation under the Protection of Wrecks Act 1973. Membership of the APWL is free and is open to all Licensees and their teams, as well as to other interested parties.

The APWL is recognised as the official voice of the Licensees and their teams and allows Licensees formal recognition by heritage bodies and representation on relevant policy bodies. The APWL provides a forum for all Licensees and team members to share ideas, views and raise issues, which can be formally expressed through the Committee. More information can be found at: www.protectedwrecks.org.uk

The APWL holds an annual meeting for Licensees (or appointed representatives), Nominated Archaeologists and team members. These meetings are usually attended by Historic England, the Government's Archaeological Contractor and Members of the HWP. These meetings provide a valuable opportunity to discuss views about work on designated wrecks and to make contact with other Licensees and their Nominated Archaeologists.

Figure 11: Non-intrusive survey work on HMS *Invincible*.
Image: Michael Pitts and Pascoe Archaeology Service

2 Planning a Project

This section offers guidance on how to plan your project. Applying for different types of licenced access will require different levels of planning. Please note that any work that disturbs the sea bed or involves the recovery of artefacts will require a full Project Design to accompany the application form.

2.1 Site ownership, location and administrative responsibility

Some historic shipwrecks have an identifiable owner, particularly if they were naval or East India Company vessels. Of the current Protected Wreck Sites in English waters, about a fifth are owned by the Ministry of Defence, while almost three-fifths do not currently have a recorded owner. The remaining sites are largely owned by private individuals or by Trusts. However, title to personal effects of people on board will normally lie with the beneficiaries of each individual's estate. Cargos may also have separate, identifiable owners. Under the *Merchant Shipping Act* 1995, ownership is usually vested in the Crown if the original owners cannot be traced.

It is important to recognise in England that the seabed within which a wreck lies is owned and administered; the administrator would normally be The Crown Estate, but it may also be the National Trust or another land-owning body. As a general rule, The Crown Estate encourages legitimate use of the foreshore and this would probably extend to the seabed. Any intrusive investigations or the fixing of equipment to the seabed will usually require Crown Estate consent in addition to consent from other regulatory bodies.

In addition, some sites are located in areas where navigational and administrative responsibility lies with a Harbour Authority. Such areas are clearly marked on Navigational Charts and local by-laws may be in force to ensure navigational safety. Licensees are expected to make contact with owners and appropriate authorities, where known.

2.2 Intrusive and non-intrusive investigation

All activities undertaken on Protected Wreck Sites must comply with accepted standards of archaeological investigation. It is also recommended that projects are compatible with, and reflect, Historic England's *Conservation Principles for the Sustainable Management of the Historic Environment* and its published policies and guidelines, as well as with the wider statutory and policy framework, inclusive of the *UK Marine Policy Statement.*

The investigation of archaeological sites can be separated into non-intrusive and intrusive activities. Non-intrusive activities include measured and geophysical survey, drawing, photography, note-taking or even simply visiting a site. Intrusive investigations can range from geotechnical (bore-hole) surveys, evaluation and excavation, to other interventions, such as recovering artefacts exposed on the site, probing and sampling.

All intrusive investigations are destructive to a greater or lesser extent. Every time a part of a

Figure 12: The recovery of the rudder from the Swash Channel Wreck site.
Image: Bournemouth University

site is dismantled by excavation, the information in that area will no longer survive in its original form. With good archaeological techniques there will be a record kept of the sediments, the objects within them and the relationship between the finds and the matrix in which they are held. This 'preservation by record' is only of use if the records are detailed, well ordered and stored in a suitable archive where others can have access to them in the future.

A site destroyed by excavation is irreplaceable. There are a finite number of historic wrecks in the sea and it is therefore important to consider whether excavation is necessary, or whether investigation should wait for some time in the future when, inevitably, new techniques may enable fuller investigation without disturbing the site. Most buried sites will last almost indefinitely if left undisturbed.

At the outset of a proposed marine project on a Protected Wreck Site where material is proposed for recovery, owners (where known) and project participants should be asked to sign a waiver recognising the requirement to report wreck material to the Receiver of Wreck foregoing any claim, and foregoing any claim to non-wreck material. Also, discussion of the deposition of material should be undertaken to include the Receiver of Wreck as well as the potential receiving museum, although it is recognised that the final deposition of wreck material cannot be agreed until the legal process of establishing ownership has taken place.

Intrusive investigations are also more demanding in terms of finance, time, commitment, expertise, conservation and publication.

Because of the potential complexity and the potential destruction of archaeological evidence, applications for intrusive work, Figure 13, on Protected Wreck Sites have to be considered extremely carefully before a licence is issued.

Thought should be given to the preliminary dissemination of results and data, where appropriate. Some organisations already publish assessment reports – usually on-line – so that useful or significant data is made available in advance of analysis (see Section 4 for more information).

2.3 Dive Trails

Historic England's strategy for making the past part of the future includes fostering a dynamic heritage cycle of understanding, valuing, caring and enjoying the historic environment. Maritime archaeology is often by its very nature inaccessible, lying deep beneath the waves and out of sight of the majority of the population. This means that is it vital to engage audiences with maritime archaeology through specific education and outreach programmes designed to raise the profile of our shared submerged cultural heritage. By making the results of research widely available it is possible to increase knowledge and understanding, attract new visitors, and prompt new questions to ensure that the historic environment is placed high in the consciousness of future generations. Dive trails are one mechanism that enables this to be achieved.

Dive trails provide interpretation material and enhanced access by licensed visiting divers. Historic England benefits from increased visitors to these sites as divers are encouraged to share with us photos taken on their visits which can enable site monitoring (for Heritage at Risk purposes) while the additional presence of licensed divers on site can act as a deterrent to anyone thinking of illegally accessing the wrecks.

There are additional surprising secondary benefits too; it has long been established that the heritage values of wreck sites can also provide social and economic benefits through being utilised as a learning or recreational resource or as a generator of tourism.

Research commissioned by Historic England, and undertaken by the Nautical Archaeology Society, has also demonstrated that diver trails have local economic benefits too (over and above heritage values) which demonstrate the importance of underwater heritage and tourism as a contribution to the growth agenda – a fact recognised by all UK Governments. For example, the diver trail on the Protected Wreck *Coronation* (in the Plymouth area) was worth £42,557 to the local economy in 2012 alone.

If you are thinking about installing a dive trail on a protected wreck site, the first step is to discuss the proposal with Historic England.

Figure 13: A diver about to experience the *Iona II* dive trail using an underwater guide book.
Image: Wessex Archaeology, © Crown Copyright.

Case Study

The trail on HMS *Colossus* is a good example of a successful dive trail. *Colossus* was a 74-gun third rate ship-of-the-line built at Gravesend, and launched in 1787. Her last naval engagement was at the Battle of Cape St Vincent (1797), during the course of which she was badly damaged. The **Colossus** was stripped of her stores to repair the serving ships, and ordered to return to England, carrying wounded from the battle, along with prize items and part of a collection of Greek antiquities amassed by Sir William Hamilton. The *Colossus* approached the Channel in December 1798 but came aground on Southward Well Rocks in the Isles of Scilly. The stern section of the *Colossus* was designated in 2001 and the site includes a large section of ship structure, cannon and, among other items, muskets, mizzen chains and a rudder gudgeon. There is still large amount to see on the seabed and it was realised that this would make a site that would be of great interest to visiting divers.

Funding from Historic England enabled the Cornwall and Isles of Scilly Maritime Archaeology Society to plan and to install a dive trail on *Colossus*. Divers visiting the site are given a briefing about the site and what they can expect to see by a local boat skipper before they enter the water. They are also given an underwater guide book, below, which guides them around a trail of numbered seabed stations that highlight interesting features.

Figure 14: A visiting diver explores the *Colossus* using an underwater guide book.
Image: CISMAS

2.4 Fieldwork safety

All activities taking place under licence should avoid unnecessary risks and must conform to recognised safe operational practices. It is therefore a condition of all licences that fieldwork is carried out to recognised safety standards. The Licensee has a responsibility to ensure that all authorised activities on a Protected Wreck Site are undertaken in a manner that is both safe and appropriate. In line with the main diving training agencies, Historic England will not endorse solo diving procedures.

Recreational diving organisations have published guidance on safe diving practices and guidance on Risk Assessment for diving which aim to place emphasis on the prevention of incidents while promoting safe diving practices to all divers. General advice on diving safety is also available from the British Diving Safety Group (BDSG).

For vessel safety, the Combined Diving Associations have produced *Guidelines for the Safe Operation of Member Club Dive Boats* (see www.bsac.com) and the BDSG have published *Advice to Divers Chartering Dive Boats* (see www.bdsg.org). However, it must be remembered that Small Vessels operating commercially under the British Flag or in British waters must comply with the Merchant Shipping Regulations or an appropriate MCA Code of Practice.

As a minimum, it is also recommended that team members who work on vessels undertake Personal Survival Training or the RYA Small Craft Basic Sea Survival course and be familiar with appropriate emergency radio procedures. First Aid, Oxygen Administration and RYA Boat Handling qualifications should also be considered.

For those diving at work, the *Health and Safety at Work Act* 1974 forms the basis for much of the legislation covering health and safety at work.

The main set of regulations that apply to diving are the *Diving at Work Regulations* 1997. These regulations cover all dives when one or more divers are at work and seek to control the hazards and risks associated with diving. Guidance offered by the *Health and Safety Executive's (HSE) Diving at Work Regulations* 1997 defines a diver as 'a person at work who dives'. This phrase covers divers who dive as part of their duties as an employee, but diving does not have to be the main activity of the employee.

All divers at work must hold an approved diving qualification suitable for the work they intend to do. A list of current approved qualifications can be obtained from the HSE; employed divers without an HSE approved qualification will not be considered competent to dive as a nominated member of a dive team.

The Health and Safety Executive has produced a set of five *Approved Codes of Practice* (ACOPs), one for each of the different sectors of the commercial

Figure 15: All team members should conform to recognised safe operating practices.
Image: Luke Mair

```
┌─────────────────────────────────────────────┐
│   Applicants apply for and secure a licence under   │
│        the Protection of Wrecks Act 1973            │
└─────────────────────────────────────────────┘
           ↙                              ↘
┌──────────────────────────────┐  ┌──────────────────────────────┐
│ At the point the PWA licence │  │ PWA Licensee applies directly│
│ is issued HE inform the MMO  │  │ to the MMO for a licence     │
│ that it will shortly receive │  │ under the Marine and Coastal │
│ an application from a PWA    │  │ Access Act 2009              │
│ licensed team                │  │                              │
└──────────────────────────────┘  └──────────────────────────────┘
```

Figure 16: The process for applying for licences under both the *Protection of Wrecks Act* 1973 and the *Marine and Coastal Access Act* 2009.

---

diving industry. The ACOPs give advice on meeting the requirements of the *Diving at Work Regulations* 1997. Further information on diving at work, including free diving information sheets, is available from the HSE:
www.hse.gov.uk/diving/index.htm

The Scientific Diving Supervisory Committee (SDSC) is the recognised representative body for the Scientific and Archaeological sector with regard to the Diving at Work regulations. Further information on the SDSC is available online at:
www.uk-sdsc.com

Figure 17: Protected Wreck Sites can be home for marine wildlife.
Image: Wessex Archaeology, © Crown Copyright.

2.5 Environmental considerations

The *Marine and Coastal Access Act* 2009 introduced a new system of marine management and established an independent body, the Marine Management Organisation (MMO) which regulates marine activities in the seas around England and Wales.

Through its regulatory activities, the MMO administers a marine licensing system that covers a broad range of activities, inclusive of projects directed at historic or archaeological sites, as described in section 66 of the 2009 Act.

Section 69 of the 2009 Act details how the MMO (as appropriate licensing authority) in determining an application must have regard to 'the need to protect the marine environment'.

This is defined in section 115(2) as inclusive of "any site (including and site comprising, or comprising the remains of, any vessel, aircraft or marine structure) which is of historic or archaeological interest". Historic England therefore acknowledges that activities (as described in section 66 and not subject to any exemption order) directed at seabed historic or archaeological sites will require a licence from the MMO; this includes some activities on Protected Wreck Sites.

The *UK Marine Policy Statement*, jointly published by all UK Administrations in 2011, recognises the need to protect and manage marine cultural heritage according to its significance. In order for the MMO to determine the significance of seabed historic or archaeological sites, Historic England is the primary advisor to the MMO for all marine works requiring consent that affect the marine historic environment under the Marine Licensing system in England. Historic England's advice is given to the MMO:

- without prejudice

- within the framework of the Rules annexed to the 2001 *Unesco Convention on the Protection of Underwater Cultural Heritage*

- within the framework of the *UK Marine Policy Statement*, **and**

- within the framework of *Conservation Principles*, which can be summarised as follows:

    - the historic environment is a shared resource

    - everyone should be able to participate in sustaining the historic environment

    - understanding the significance of places is vital

    - significant places should be managed to sustain their values

    - decisions about change must be reasonable, transparent and consistent, **and**

    - documenting and learning from decisions is essential

If you are planning to undertake an archaeological project on a Protected Wreck Site that is likely to involve excavation and/or deposition, Historic England encourage you to contact the MMO before you submit a marine licence application.

The MMO will advise you on the level of pre-application preparation required, as it will depend on what you propose to do. For example, it might be sufficient to look at the main issues governing underwater and foreshore archaeology combined with the need to address other issues as relevant to marine licensing (eg navigation safety, natural habitat protection etc) and they will help you to deal with those issues relevant to your application.

For more information please see *Marine Licensing and the Historic Environment*.

Historic England strongly advises you to consult with the Marine Management Organisation (MMO) before submitting a marine licence application for projects aimed at underwater and foreshore archaeology on Protected Wreck Sites.

All legal requirements to report 'wreck' as defined by the *Merchant Shipping Act* 1995 remain applicable in addition to securing any marine licence consent.

Additional consent is likely to be necessary in the case of sites within the jurisdiction of a Port or Harbour Authority, and the appropriate authority should be consulted.

2.6 Funding and training

Although the *National Heritage Act* 2002 enables Historic England to grant-aid archaeological work below the low water mark, this opportunity must be balanced against the Historic England Action Plan which sets out how Historic England together with partners in the heritage sector will prioritise and deliver heritage protection from 2011 to 2015.

Other sources of project funding should also be considered. For example, grants are available from the British Academy (the national academy for the humanities and the social sciences) to support archaeological fieldwork, together with related general and scientific post-excavation work (see www.britac.ac.uk for more information).

Project funding can also be sought from the Heritage Lottery Fund (HLF), which distributes a share of the income from the National Lottery to projects aimed at preserving and making accessible the nation's heritage. Each of the English regions has its own dedicated HLF team and decision-making committees (see www.hlf.org.uk for more information).

> The sale of antiquities recovered from a Protected Wreck Site is not to be considered as a potential source of project funding. If a wreck is sufficiently important to warrant designation, then the material archive (finds) should be kept together in a publicly accessible place for the benefit of present and future generations. Licences will not be issued simply to allow the recovery of objects for dispersal.

Depending on the nature of a proposed project, appropriate training may be necessary for successful licence applications. The Department of Culture, Media and Sport attaches great importance to appropriate training in archaeological techniques and encourages applicants, Licensees and their teams to attend courses available from a number of organisations involved in promoting nautical archaeology, in the first instance.

2.7 Producing a Project Design

The Project Design sets out the academic justification for the proposed project. It will usually be multi-authored, with specialists in each area contributing as required.

> **Project Designs** are considered necessary for all licence applications for work that disturbs the sea bed or involves the recovery of artefacts

The more relevant information that is provided within a Project Design, the easier it is for Historic England and DCMS to understand exactly what is proposed. The Project Design should set out the plan for the fieldwork and include all standards to be met and all processes that will be used. Developing a Project Design is straightforward and advice can be sought from Historic England. Some types of licence require a Nominated Archaeologist to be part of the team and it is important that they are involved in the preparation of the Project Design.

Thorough guidance for the preparation of a Project Design is given in Appendix 1 and in *The MoRPHE Project Managers Guide*. However, the following elements will always need to be addressed:

- Project background

- Aims and objectives

- Method statement

- Resources and programming

- Safety statement

3 During a Project

3.1 Fieldwork: data collection

Archaeological investigation encompasses an increasing variety of activities and techniques, with different types of projects having different means of collecting data and assessing value and significance, and achieving increased understanding. However, each project will share a number of key stages: data collection and assessment, analysis, understanding, and dissemination. Each of these 'Execution Stages' are defined in more detail in Historic England's *MoRPHE Project Planning Note: Archaeological Excavation* and *MoRPHE Project Planning Note: Marine Investigation*, but it is important to note that each Stage must be subject to continual assessment and review, which is essential for the successful achievement of each component and for the project as a whole.

As the value of the knowledge gained is entirely dependent on the quality of the fieldwork, it is important that every team member is able to competently undertake any task allocated to him or her. Similarly, it is essential that all team members understand their role in the project and are familiar with project documentation, such as the Project Design.

Figure 18: A diver records archaeology on the seabed.
Image: Wessex Archaeology, © Crown Copyright.

Figure 19: Work on the Swash Channel designated wreck discovered this carved merman.
Image: Bournemouth University.

3.2 Dealing with finds

Surface recovery and excavation is likely to generate archaeological material (finds) (Figure 20). This raises a number of important issues:

- A marine licence under the *Marine and Coastal Access Act* 2009 may be required for such recoveries

- There is a legal requirement to report the recovery of material to the Receiver of Wreck, under the terms of the *Merchant Shipping Act* 1995

- Recovered material will require conservation

- Permanent deposition and curation of artefacts must be arranged

Any wreck material found in UK territorial waters (to a 12-mile limit), or outside the UK and brought within UK territorial waters, must by law be reported to the Receiver of Wreck (under section 236 of the *Merchant Shipping Act* 1995). Finders should assume that all recovered material has an owner.

The rights to items of wreck lie firstly with the owner. The Receiver will seek archaeological advice as to the identity, age and importance of historic finds. If no owner is found within a year, the Crown becomes the owner and then the law allows the item to be disposed of legally. In cases of historically or archaeologically important material, such as that recovered from Protected Wreck Sites, the Maritime and Coastguard Agency has a policy of placing such material in registered repositories where the public can access them.

Figure 20: Archaeological finds should be kept wet and not allowed to dry out at any stage

It should be noted that Historic England encourages Licensees to waive their rights to a salvage award (under the *Merchant Shipping Act* 1995) in favour of an appropriate museum in recognition of the historic, artistic or archaeological importance of the site, consistent with advice given in *Our Portable Past.*

Historic England has issued guidelines on the first aid treatment and conservation management of finds recovered from protected wreck sites in the guide Caring for our Shipwreck Heritage. Guidance on caring for a range of objects and materials is also available from the Institute of Conservation (www.icon.org.uk), as is the Conservation Register: a service that provides information on accredited conservator-restorers in the UK. Guidance may also be sought from Historic England's Conservation Department.

The necessary conservation facilities need to be planned in advance of any licence application involving artefact recovery and the expertise of a recognised conservation laboratory or an accredited conservator will need to be arranged and confirmed by them in writing. It is extremely important to manage and control the records relating to the site and its objects carefully and to ensure that records are made available in a publicly accessible archive.

With regard to recovered objects, all Licensees are required to do the following:

Keep it wet ➔ Waterlogged material must not be allowed to dry out. Irreversible loss will occur that may render the artefact worthless for future study.

Keep it dark ➔ Reduced light levels or ideally, dark storage will hinder microbiological growth and keep temperatures down.

Keep it cool ➔ Reduced temperatures will slow decay rates down and hinder microbiological growth. Fridges, cool boxes or cooling porta-cabins are suitable. Freezing is only recommended as a last resort and in consultation with a conservator. Artefacts will suffer physical damage if they are not stored correctly and subjected to uncontrolled freeze-thaw cycles over the winter.

Monitor it ➔ Routinely monitor the condition of the artefacts, packaging and the water levels. Establish procedures to respond if the condition deteriorates including informing project manager, conservator and finds specialist.

Figure 21: A diver recovers environmental samples from the *Royal Anne* Galley.
Image: Kevin Camidge

3.3 Environmental archaeology

For Protected Wreck Sites, sampling to recover environmental materials is usually aimed at understanding the vessel (date, construction, re-fit, and repair), the nature of life on board (cargo and supplies), and the post-wreck environment. Different sampling strategies will be required to fulfil these aims: for example wood samples for dendrochronology and wood analysis, samples from deposits within the vessel or objects from it, or samples for geoarchaeological analysis from within and around the vessel. As sampling usually requires an excavation licence, it needs to be detailed in a Project Design and the following points should be addressed:

- the reason for sampling
- the size, likely number and location of samples required
- the level of disturbance involved
- the sampling procedure
- the resources and equipment needed for processing
- the nature of the analysis proposed
- details of the institution or individuals who have agreed to carry out the analysis, together with their written acknowledgement, **and**
- the possible impact of the disturbance on the site or its surrounding environment

Further advice in is available from Historic England's Environmental Studies team and Science Advisors. For further information on environmental archaeology, geoarchaeology and dendrochronology see the following publications:

Environmental Archaeology: a guide to the theory and practice of methods, from sampling to post-excavation (second edition, 2011).

Dendrochronology: guidelines on producing and interpreting dendrochronological dates (1998)

Geoarchaeology: using earth sciences to understand the archaeological record (2007)

3.4 Site Security and liaison

Under the terms of the *Protection of Wrecks Act* 1973, it is a criminal offence to do any of the following in a designated area without a licence granted by the appropriate Secretary of State:

- tamper with, damage or remove any part of a vessel lying wrecked on or in the seabed or any object formerly contained in such a vessel
- carry out diving or salvage operations directed to the exploration of any wreck or to removing objects from it or from the seabed, or use equipment constructed or adapted for any purpose of diving or salvage operations, **and**
- deposit, so as to fall and lie abandoned on the sea bed, anything that, if it were to fall on the site of a wreck (whether it so falls or not), would wholly or partly obliterate the site or obstruct access to it, or damage any part of the wreck

It is also an offence to permit any of these things to be done by others in a restricted area, other than under the authority of such a licence. Where a person is authorised by a licence to access the site, it is an offence for any other person to obstruct them, or cause or permit them to be obstructed, in doing anything that is authorised by the licence.

Bathing, angling and navigation are permitted within a restricted area provided there is no likelihood of, or intention to, damage the wreck or obstruct work on it. Anchoring on the site is only permitted for licensed activities or in cases of maritime distress. In some cases the presence of a site is indicated by a buoy, usually yellow and inscribed 'Protected Wreck' (Figure 22). Suitably placed notices sometimes indicate sites close to the shore. Some are warning signs; and others are public information notices giving a brief explanation of why the wreck is important and a description of the site.

Figure 22: The Yarmouth Roads Wreck is clearly marked by a yellow buoy.

Any suspicion of unauthorised access to a Protected Wreck Site should be reported to the relevant local Police Service, Maritime and Coastguard Agency and Historic England.

You should call **999** when a crime is in progress or someone suspected of a crime is nearby. Where you believe that an offence may have been committed and the suspect is no longer at the scene you should call the Police using the national non-emergency number 101.

If you have information about a crime relating to an protected wreck but you do not wish to be a witness you can pass on your information to Crimestoppers by calling 0800 555 111. The service is confidential and you will not be asked for your name or personal details.

All reports of unauthorised access will be fully investigated.

All Protected Wreck Sites are listed in an annual *Admiralty Notice to Mariners* (ANM12) and published in *Admiralty Sailing Directions*. Further, the locations of restricted areas are readily available as they are clearly marked and annotated on Admiralty Charts, the Government's Multi-Agency Geographic Information system for the Countryside website (www.magic.gov.uk) and available as GIS shapefile downloads from Historic England's website. In addition, Statutory Instruments setting out the designation details of individual sites are available from the Office of Public Sector Information (www.opsi.org).

Licensees are encouraged to establish relationships with marine enforcement agencies (such as local Coastguard officers, Marine Police Units and Inshore Fisheries and Conservation Authority officers) in order to facilitate and promote site security. National Coastwatch Institutions should also be contacted to assist with the recognition of authorised vessels and the identification of unauthorised sea-users. In all cases, Historic England can advise on contact details upon request.

The Alliance to Reduce Crime Against Heritage (ARCH) is a voluntary national network which will take forward initiatives to tackle heritage crime and galvanise local action as part of the Heritage Crime Programme. The overriding objective of the group is to reduce the amount of crime that causes damage to or interferes with the enjoyment of heritage assets in England. Members of ARCH have a shared interest in preventing and seeing effective enforcement of heritage crime. Membership of the group is free and open to all organisations and groups that have an interest in preventing and enforcing heritage crime; Licensee's and their teams are strongly encouraged to become members.

If you are interested in finding out more about the Heritage Crime Programme, or becoming a member of ARCH, please contact Historic England's Customer Services Department:
customers@HistoricEngland.org.uk

3.5 Monitoring and site restitution

It is accepted that all wreck sites are vulnerable simply because of the nature of their environment. Licensees should therefore monitor and record the effect that authorised activities have on the stability of sites and should seek advice if erosion is observed or deterioration of exposed material begins to accelerate.

Historic England has developed a risk assessment methodology in order to both identify and manage risks to historic wreck sites which includes a single-page checklist which Licensees can use to record annual change to individual sites.

Any equipment that the Licensee wishes to deploy on a Protected Wreck Site should be described, before its use, in the licence application or annual Licensee's report. Licensees should be prepared to remove unwanted material at the end of any period of organised work especially if it is uncertain whether work will take place the following season.

Material abandoned on Protected Wreck Sites in the past includes scaffold poles from surveys and evaluation trenches; steel diver-support structures and platforms; sheet steel piling; airlift manifolds and air-lines; survey and mooring ropes/lines; concrete and iron weights used for survey points or moorings and steel rods used as datum points. Such debris can cause scouring, trap drifting debris, accelerate erosion and affect the viability of any site stabilisation measures.

4 Reporting, Archiving and Dissemination

4.1 Submitting Licensee reports

In order for a Protected Wreck Site to be managed in accordance with its significance, it is essential that the licensing authority receives accurate reports on authorised activities. Licensees are therefore required to submit a report, signed by the Licensee and the Nominated Archaeologist (where appropriate), to Historic England by the date specified in the licence conditions. These reports are discussed further in Appendix 3. Licensees should be aware that annual reports form part of the public archive of each site.

> **Licensees** are expected to formally report any instances of unauthorised access to Protected Wreck Sites to both the local Constabulary and Historic England.

It is a condition of all licences that a report is submitted to Historic England and the Historic England Archive. The purpose of the report is to keep Historic England and DCMS informed about what is happening on the sites for which they have a responsibility. It also gives them information that can inform site management decisions.

> Licences will **not** be renewed if a Licensee fails to submit a report.

Reports should contain information about the quality and outcomes of the project and requirements will vary between, for example, a licence issued to allow a site visit and a licence issued to undertake a major research based excavation. A guide to a suggested format is set out in Appendix 3.

The Nominated Archaeologist, where there is one, must countersign all reports. If the licence is to be renewed the report should also state what your intentions are, although a revised Project Design will be necessary if a new research question or a new project is to be pursued. If an archaeologist is going to be required for the next phase of work, then their willingness to collaborate must be indicated by their signature on the application.

The investigation of Protected Wreck Sites can reveal significant information and licences are issued on the understanding that resulting information will be made available to others (forming part of the public archive for the site). This requirement can be achieved in a variety of ways, including short reports in a newsletter, published conference proceedings, full articles in academic journals, or even in separate publications.

A standard condition of licences requires that a report of the investigation be submitted to Historic England. The report will be lodged with the Historic England Archive and may be made available to the wider community on-line through the Historic England website. Licensees and their archaeologists are also encouraged to produce popular accounts of their work that might appeal to a wider audience. Advice on how to set about publishing can be obtained from Historic England.

4.2 The project archive

All archaeological investigations will generate an archive, which will generally consist of the paper, artefact and environmental archive and the evaluation report. These materials should be submitted to the relevant archive repository to an agreed timetable, as identified in the Project Design. In addition, a summary of the work must be submitted to the local Historic Environment Record, and an OASIS form completed (where appropriate), which will provide a summary of the work and the location of the archive. These steps are required of all evaluations, even if the results are negative or unlikely to lead to subsequent work.

Original drawings, photographs and measurements, together with details of research and geophysical survey data, form the essential part of the site archive. It is important to keep all information about the site in one place, and store it in an orderly way. The archive must be accessible to the Nominated Archaeologist and, ideally, to all the team members. At the end of the project a copy of the archive must be offered to a suitable public repository, with a view to its being made publicly available. Suitable repositories include the Historic Environment Record of the local county or the National Record of the Historic Environment (NRHE). A catalogue of the contents of a site archive should be made available to the appropriate heritage agency. Where copyright is retained by the Licensee in respect of any information relating to the site, the Licensee will normally be expected to authorise the use of that information by others for non-commercial purposes, including teaching, research and private study.

Further information on archives is given in Archaeological Archives: a guide to best practice in creation, compilation, transfer and curation (Brown 2011). Archive deposition must be planned as part of the dissemination strategy, including the deposition of electronic datasets with an appropriate digital archiving repository, such as the Archaeology Data Service (ADS).

4.3 Publication

Many Licensees expand their reports to produce publications intended for a wider audience. You do not have to be a formally trained archaeologist to have something published about a site. If it is clearly written, well-illustrated and brings interesting facts to light, then it stands a good chance of being accepted for publication. Letting people know about the work being carried out on Protected Wreck Sites is an important part of maritime archaeology, and it can be as rewarding as the archaeological investigations of the site itself and the associated historical research.

The method of publication can be as a short report in a newsletter, a full article in a journal or a separate publication in its own right. Licensees and their archaeologists are also encouraged to produce popular accounts of the work that might appeal to a wider audience. Alternative forms of dissemination such as websites, public lectures or presentations are also encouraged.

Licensees are requested to submit an annual summary report of archaeological work undertaken to a relevant county archaeological journal.

5 Where to Get Advice

Anyone may apply for a historic wreck site to be designated under the terms of the *Protection of Wrecks Act* 1973; application forms can be filled in on-line on Historic England's website: http://historicengland.org.uk/advice/planning/consents/protected-wreck-sites/applying-for-licensing/

A copy of the *Protection of Wrecks Act* 1973 can be obtained from www.opsi.gov.uk.

Further information on Protected Wreck Sites and England's Maritime Archaeology is available from the Historic England website: http://historicengland.org.uk/advice/planning/consents/protected-wreck-sites/

5.1 References and further reading

Brown, D 2011 *Archaeological Archives: a guide to best practice in creation, compilation, transfer and curation.* Reading: Chartered Institute for Archaeologists

Bowens, A, et al (eds) 2008 *Underwater Archaeology: the NAS Guide to Principles and Practice.* Oxford: WileyBlackwell

Chartered Institute for Archaeologists 2014 *Bylaws of the IFA:* Code of Conduct. Reading: Chartered Institute for Archaeologists

Dromgoole, S 1999 *Legal Protection of the Underwater Cultural Heritage: National and International Perspectives.* The Hague: Kluwer Law International

English Heritage 2006 *Taking to the Water.* Swindon: English Heritage

English Heritage 2008a *Conservation Principles, Policies and Guidance, for the Sustainable Management of the Historic Environment.* Swindon: English Heritage
https://www.historicengland.org.uk/images-books/publications/conservation-principles-sustainable-management-historic-environment/

English Heritage *2008b Protected Wreck Sites at Risk: A Risk Management Handbook.* Swindon: English Heritage
http://www.historicengland.org.uk/images-books/publications/protected-wreck-sites-at-risk-handbook/

English Heritage 2011 *Environmental Archaeology: a guide to the theory and practice of methods, from sampling to post-excavation.* 2nd edition. Swindon: English Heritage
https://www.historicengland.org.uk/images-books/publications/environmental-archaeology-2nd/

English Heritage 2012a *Caring for our Shipwreck Heritage: Guidelines on the first aid treatment and conservation management of finds recovered from designated wreck sites resulting from licensed investigations.* Swindon: English Heritage
http://historicengland.org.uk/images-books/publications/caring-shipwreck-heritage/

English Heritage 2012b *Ships and Boats; Prehistory to Present – Designation Selection Guide.* Swindon: English Heritage
http://historicengland.org.uk/images-books/publications/dsg-ships-boats/

English Heritage 2012c *Ships and Boats; 1840 - 1950 – Introduction to Heritage Assets.* Swindon: English Heritage
http://historicengland.org.uk/images-books/publications/iha-ships-boats-1840-1950/

English Heritage 2012d *Ships and Boats; Prehistory to 1840 – Introduction to Heritage Assets.* Swindon: English Heritage
http://historicengland.org.uk/images-books/publications/iha-ships-boats/

English Heritage 2014 *Our Portable Past.* Swindon: English Heritage https://www.historicengland.org.uk/images-books/publications/ourportablepast/

Historic England 2015a *Marine Licensing and the Historic Environment.* Swindon: Historic England
http://historicengland.org.uk/images-books/publications/marine-licensing-and-englands-historic-environment/

Historic England 2015b *Management of Research Projects in the Historic Environment: The MoRPHE Project Managers' Guide.* Swindon: Historic England
www.historicengland.org.uk/advice/technical-advice/project-management-for-heritage

Nautical Archaeology Society 2009 *Benchmarking Competence Requirements and Training Opportunities related to Maritime Archaeology.* Portsmouth: Nautical Archaeology Society
http://www.nauticalarchaeologysociety.org/content/benchmarking-competency-maritime-archaeology

Nautical Archaeology Society 2013 *The Local Economic Value of a Protected wreck.* Portsmouth: Nautical Archaeology Society
http://www.nauticalarchaeologysociety.org/content/local-economic-benefit-protected-wreck

Robinson W 1998 *First Aid for Marine finds.* London: Archetype Press/Nautical Archaeology Society

UNESCO 2001 *Convention on the Protection of the Underwater Cultural Heritage*. Paris: UNESCO

5.2 Useful contacts

Department of Culture Media & Sport (DCMS)
100 Parliament Street
London   SW1A 2BQ
020 7211 6000
www.culture.gov.uk

Historic England
1 Waterhouse Square
138–142 Holborn
London   EC1N 2ST
02392 856735
www.HistoricEngland.org.uk

The Receiver of Wreck
Maritime and Coastguard Agency
Spring Place
105 Commercial Road
Southampton   SO1 1EG
023 8032 9474
www.mcga.gov.uk

Ministry of Defence
CNS Heritage section
Room 123/125
South Office Block PP60
HMNB Portsmouth   PO1 3LU
www.mod.uk/defenceinternet/home

Nautical Archaeology Society
Fort Cumberland
Fort Cumberland Road
Eastney
Portsmouth   PO4 9LD
023 92818419
www.nauticalarchaeologysociety.org

Chartered Institute for Archaeologists
Miller Building
University of Reading
Reading   RG6 6AB
0118 378 6446
www.archaeologists.net

Association of Local Government Archaeological Officers (ALGAO)
Maritime Committee
c/o Robin Daniels
Tees Archaeology
Sir William Gray House
Clarence Road
Hartlepool   TS24 8BT
01429 523455/6
www.algao.org.uk

Health and Safety Executive (HSE)
Diving Operations Strategy Team
Redwing House
Hedgerows business Park
Colchester Road
Springfield
Chelmsford
Tel. 01245 706234
www.hse.gov.uk/diving/index.htm

The British Diving Safety Group
West Quay Road
Poole   BH15 1HZ
0800 328 0600
www.bdsg.org

Natural England
Block B, Government Buildings
Whittington Road
Worcester   WR5 2LQ
0300 060 3900
www.naturalengland.org.uk

Marine Management Organisation (MMO)
Lancaster House
Hampshire Court
Newcastle upon Tyne   NE4 7YH
0300 123 1032
www.marinemanagement.org.uk

5.3 Useful acronyms

ARCH	Alliance to Reduce Crime Against Heritage
DCMS	Department of Culture Media & Sport
HE	Historic England
HER	Historic Environment Record
HSE	Health and Safety Executive
IFCA	Inshore Fisheries and Conservation Authority
MCZ	Marine Conservation Zone
MMO	Marine Management Organisation
NHLE	National Heritage List for England
NRHE	National Record of the Historic Environment
NAS	Nautical Archaeology Society
PWA	*Protection of Wrecks Act* (1973)
RoW	Receiver of Wreck

6 Appendices

6.1 Annex to the 2001 UNESCO Convention on the Protection of the Underwater Cultural Heritage

Rules concerning activities directed at underwater cultural heritage.

I   General principles

Rule 1: The protection of underwater cultural heritage through in situ preservation shall be considered as the first option. Accordingly, activities directed at underwater cultural heritage shall be authorized in a manner consistent with the protection of that heritage, and subject to that requirement may be authorized for the purpose of making a significant contribution to protection or knowledge or enhancement of underwater cultural heritage.

Rule 2: The commercial exploitation of underwater cultural heritage for trade or speculation or its irretrievable dispersal is fundamentally incompatible with the protection and proper management of underwater cultural heritage. Underwater cultural heritage shall not be traded, sold, bought or bartered as commercial goods.

This Rule cannot be interpreted as preventing:

(a)   the provision of professional archaeological services or necessary services incidental thereto whose nature and purpose are in full conformity with this Convention and are subject to the authorization of the competent authorities;

(b)   the deposition of underwater cultural heritage, recovered in the course of a research project in conformity with this Convention, provided such deposition does not prejudice the scientific or cultural interest or integrity of the recovered material or result in its irretrievable dispersal; is in accordance with the provisions of Rules 33 and 34; and is subject to the authorization of the competent authorities.

Rule 3: Activities directed at underwater cultural heritage shall not adversely affect the underwater cultural heritage more than is necessary for the objectives of the project.

Rule 4: Activities directed at underwater cultural heritage must use non-destructive techniques and survey methods in preference to recovery of objects. If excavation or recovery is necessary for the purpose of scientific studies or for the ultimate protection of the underwater cultural heritage, the methods and techniques used must be as non-destructive as possible and contribute to the preservation of the remains.

Rule 5: Activities directed at underwater cultural heritage shall avoid the unnecessary disturbance of human remains or venerated sites.

Rule 6: Activities directed at underwater cultural heritage shall be strictly regulated to ensure proper recording of cultural, historical and archaeological information.

Rule 7: Public access to in situ underwater cultural heritage shall be promoted, except where such access is incompatible with protection and management.

Rule 8: International cooperation in the conduct of activities directed at underwater cultural heritage shall be encouraged in order to further the effective exchange or use of archaeologists and other relevant professionals.

II   Project design

Rule 9: Prior to any activity directed at underwater cultural heritage, a project design for the activity shall be developed and submitted to the competent authorities for authorization and appropriate peer review.

Rule 10: The project design shall include:

(a) an evaluation of previous or preliminary studies

(b) the project statement and objectives

(c) the methodology to be used and the techniques to be employed

(d) the anticipated funding

(e) an expected timetable for completion of the project

(f) the composition of the team and the qualifications, responsibilities and experience of each team member

(g) plans for post-fieldwork analysis and other activities

(h) a conservation programme for artefacts and the site in close cooperation with the competent authorities

(i) a site management and maintenance policy for the whole duration of the project

(j) a documentation programme

(k) a safety policy

(l) an environmental policy

(m) arrangements for collaboration with museums and other institutions, in particular scientific institutions

(n) report preparation

(o) deposition of archives, including underwater cultural heritage removed, **and**

(p) a programme for publication

Rule 11: Activities directed at underwater cultural heritage shall be carried out in accordance with the project design approved by the competent authorities.

Rule 12: Where unexpected discoveries are made or circumstances change, the project design shall be reviewed and amended with the approval of the competent authorities.

Rule 13: In cases of urgency or chance discoveries, activities directed at the underwater cultural heritage, including conservation measures or activities for a period of short duration, in particular site stabilization, may be authorized in the absence of a project design in order to protect the underwater cultural heritage.

III   Preliminary work

Rule 14: The preliminary work referred to in Rule 10 (a) shall include an assessment that evaluates the significance and vulnerability of the underwater cultural heritage and the surrounding natural environment to damage by the proposed project, and the potential to obtain data that would meet the project objectives.

Rule 15: The assessment shall also include background studies of available historical and archaeological evidence, the archaeological and environmental characteristics of the site, and the consequences of any potential intrusion for the long-term stability of the underwater cultural heritage affected by the activities.

IV Project objective, methodology and techniques

Rule 16: The methodology shall comply with the project objectives, and the techniques employed shall be as non-intrusive as possible.

V Funding

Rule 17: Except in cases of emergency to protect underwater cultural heritage, an adequate funding base shall be assured in advance of any activity, sufficient to complete all stages of the project design, including conservation, documentation and curation of recovered artefacts, and report preparation and dissemination.

Rule 18: The project design shall demonstrate an ability, such as by securing a bond, to fund the project through to completion.

Rule 19: The project design shall include a contingency plan that will ensure conservation of underwater cultural heritage and supporting documentation in the event of any interruption of anticipated funding.

VI Project duration – timetable

Rule 20: An adequate timetable shall be developed to assure in advance of any activity directed at underwater cultural heritage the completion of all stages of the project design, including conservation, documentation and curation of recovered underwater cultural heritage, as well as report preparation and dissemination.

Rule 21: The project design shall include a contingency plan that will ensure conservation of underwater cultural heritage and supporting documentation in the event of any interruption or termination of the project.

VII Competence and qualifications

Rule 22: Activities directed at underwater cultural heritage shall only be undertaken under the direction and control of, and in the regular presence of, a qualified underwater archaeologist with scientific competence appropriate to the project.

Rule 23: All persons on the project team shall be qualified and have demonstrated competence appropriate to their roles in the project.

VIII Conservation and site management

Rule 24: The conservation programme shall provide for the treatment of the archaeological remains during the activities directed at underwater cultural heritage, during transit and in the long term. Conservation shall be carried out in accordance with current professional standards.

Rule 25: The site management programme shall provide for the protection and management in situ of underwater cultural heritage, in the course of and upon termination of fieldwork. The programme shall include public information, reasonable provision for site stabilization, monitoring, and protection against interference.

IX Documentation

Rule 26: The documentation programme shall set out thorough documentation including a progress report of activities directed at underwater cultural heritage, in accordance with current professional standards of archaeological documentation.

Rule 27: Documentation shall include, at a minimum, a comprehensive record of the site, including the provenance of underwater cultural heritage moved or removed in the course of the activities directed at underwater cultural heritage, field notes, plans, drawings, sections, and photographs or recording in other media.

X Safety

Rule 28: A safety policy shall be prepared that is adequate to ensure the safety and health of the project team and third parties and that is in conformity with any applicable statutory and professional requirements.

XI Environment

Rule 29: An environmental policy shall be prepared that is adequate to ensure that the seabed and marine life are not unduly disturbed.

XII   Reporting

Rule 30: Interim and final reports shall be made available according to the timetable set out in the project design, and deposited in relevant public records.

Rule 31: Reports shall include:

(a)   an account of the objectives

(b)   an account of the methods and techniques employed

(c)   an account of the results achieved

(d)   basic graphic and photographic documentation on all phases of the activity

(e)   recommendations concerning conservation and curation of the site and of any underwater cultural heritage removed, **and**

(f)   recommendations for future activities

XIII   Curation of project archives

Rule 32: Arrangements for curation of the project archives shall be agreed to before any activity commences, and shall be set out in the project design.

Rule 33: The project archives, including any underwater cultural heritage removed and a copy of all supporting documentation shall, as far as possible, be kept together and intact as a collection in a manner that is available for professional and public access as well as for the curation of the archives. This should be done as rapidly as possible and in any case not later than ten years from the completion of the project, in so far as may be compatible with conservation of the underwater cultural heritage.

Rule 34: The project archives shall be managed according to international professional standards, and subject to the authorization of the competent authorities.

XIV   Dissemination

Rule 35: Projects shall provide for public education and popular presentation of the project results where appropriate.

Rule 36: A final synthesis of a project shall be:

(a)   made public as soon as possible, having regard to the complexity of the project and the confidential or sensitive nature of the information, **and**

(b)   deposited in relevant public records

The foregoing is the authentic text of the Convention duly adopted by the General Conference of the United Nations Educational, Scientific and Cultural Organization during its thirty-first session, which was held in Paris and declared closed the third day of November 2001.

(source: www.unesco.org/culture/laws/underwater/html_eng/conven3.shtml)

6.2 Standard licence conditions

Listed below are the standard conditions placed on licences issued for protected wreck sites in English waters. Additional conditions may be placed on licences as necessary. For example, sites with more than one active Licensee may have the following additional condition placed on the licence: The Licensee will contact Historic England prior to accessing the site.

All relevant conditions form part of the licence and it is important to note that: a licence can be revoked at any time if any of the general or specific conditions are not complied with.

1. Dives will only be permitted when a licensee is present at the site

2. The Licensee(s) on the site will be responsible for the supervision at all times of all divers participating in dives at the site

3. During the carrying out of licenced operations divers must not tamper with or damage the said Protected Wreck. No objects whatsoever may be recovered by them from the site with the exception of objects under immediate threat of significant harm or loss and only after prior consultation with and the approval of Historic England

4. Only non-intrusive dives are permitted

5. The Principal Licensee submits a report on the progress of their operations to Historic England no later than [date]

6. Diving must be carried out to an approved code of practice as indicated on the application form

7. Diving operations within the restricted area must be carried out in accordance with the application & Project Design where appropriate submitted to Historic England dated [date]

8. The Principal Licensee must deposit a copy of the archive of the project at the Historic England Archive

9. Geophysical data must be made available to all researchers in a non-proprietary format upon request ie raw xyz data: TXT, CSV

10. The Principal Licensee must obtain any necessary consents from other marine regulating bodies

11. The Principal Licensee ensures that any objects recovered from the restricted area are reported to the Receiver of Wreck under the terms of the *Merchant Shipping Act* 1995

12. The Principal Licensee ensures that any objects recovered from the restricted area are given 'first aid' conservation treatment

13. The Principal Licensee ensures that any samples recovered from the restricted area are stored appropriately

14. The Licensee(s) must ensure that all activities conform to the Rules annexed to the 2001 *Convention on the Protection of the Underwater Cultural Heritage*

15. The Principal Licensee must provide Historic England with the names of all divers diving under this licence. Names must be submitted within 2 weeks of 31 May, 31 August and 30 November during the validity of this licence

16. Anyone convicted of an offence under section 3(3) of the Act, or under comparable legislation outside England, which is not a spent offence within the meaning of section 1 of the *Rehabilitation Act* 1974 may not dive under this licence, except in exceptional circumstances and with the permission of the Secretary of State

6.3 Licensee's annual report

Archaeological reports usually follow a standard layout, namely:

- Project background
- Aims and objectives
- Methodology
- Results
- Recommendations

A suggested format for archaeological reports is given in **Rule 31** of the Annex to the UNESCO *Convention on the Protection of the Underwater Cultural Heritage* 2001 (see Appendix 1). The following format is recommended for Annual Licensee's Reports:

(a) summary

(b) an account of the project's objectives

(c) an account of the methods and techniques employed

(d) an account of the results achieved

(e) basic graphic and photographic documentation on all phases of the activity

(f) recommendations concerning conservation and curation of the site and of any underwater cultural heritage removed, **and**

(g) recommendations for future activities

A Licensee's report should not contain any discussion or comment of a personal nature that the Licensee would not wish to be part of the public site archive, as the report will be deposited with the Historic England Archive.

Where copyright remains with the Licensee (and save where confidentiality is justified), the Licensee will be expected to grant a non-exclusive licence authorising the use of the report, and any material within it, for non-commercial purposes including teaching, research and private study. In any case where confidentiality is required, this should be made clear in the report, along with the reasons for such a requirement.

The report should be as objective as possible, factual, independent, to the point and preferably typed. Wherever possible digital copies of the report are preferred.

We are the public body that looks after England's historic environment. We champion historic places, helping people understand, value and care for them.

Please contact
guidance@HistoricEngland.org.uk
with any questions about this document.

HistoricEngland.org.uk

If you would like this document in a different format, please contact our customer services department on:

Tel: 0370 333 0607
Fax: 01793 414926
Textphone: 0800 015 0174
Email: customers@HistoricEngland.org.uk

HEAG075
Publication date: August 2010 © English Heritage
Reissue date: October 2015 © Historic England
Design: Historic England

Please consider the environment before printing this document

< < Contents

Printed in France by Amazon
Brétigny-sur-Orge, FR

44881957R00027